C.S. Lewis' Little Instruction Book

A Classic Treasury of Timeless Wisdom and Reflection

Tulsa, Oklahoma

C.S. Lewis' Little Instruction Book
ISBN 1-56292-171-1
Copyright © 1997 by Honor Books, Inc.
P.O. Box 55388
Tulsa, OK 74155

Compiled by James S. Bell, Jr.

Introduction

C.S. Lewis (1898-1963) has often been called the greatest communicator of the Christian faith in this century. He combined his brilliant mind and rich imagination to defend and explain the faith in ways that continue to satisfy millions of readers today. Because of his intense struggle with spirituality as a young atheist, he was sensitive to the conflicts of others and spoke to their areas of resistance and need. Lewis carried the Christian faith into new areas, including science fiction, fairy tale, satire, and myth, to convey the truth and complexity of the gospel to others searching for answers. At the same time, he was highly respected as a literary scholar at both Oxford and Cambridge Universities in England.

His best-selling works include *Mere Christianity*, which originated from a series of radio broadcast talks; *The Screwtape Letters*, a dialogue between devils assigned to tempt a human; and *The Chronicles of Narnia*, a series of allegorical Christian fairy tales for children. His influence, both during his lifetime and after his death, both in his published work and personal contacts, is enormous and continues to grow. During his early life, he sought the experience of joy to discover God as the source. All of his works are shot through with joy and the Person of God made real in a way only His servant C.S. Lewis could demonstrate.

Note: Unless otherwise indicated, all quotations are from C.S. Lewis.

The Only Man Alive

When Christ died, He died for you individually just as much as if you had been the only man in the world.

For while we were still helpless, at the right time Christ died for the ungodly.

ROMANS 5:6

Mere Christianity

Unique Saints

Sameness is to be found most among the most "natural" men, not among those who surrender to Christ. How monotonously alike all the great tyrants and conquerors have been: how gloriously different are the saints.

The mystery that has been kept hidden for ages and generations, but is now disclosed to the saints.... the hope of glory.

COLOSSIANS 1:26,27 NIV

Mere Christianity

True personality lies ahead....We are marble waiting to be shaped, metal waiting to be run into a mould.

Uncut Marble

But now, O LORD, Thou art our Father, We are the clay, and Thou our potter; And all of us are the work of Thy hand.

ISAIAH 64:8

The Weight of Glory

Did You Know?

Though he spent most of his life in England, he grew up in Northern Ireland.

No Need For Modesty?

Perfect humility dispenses with modesty.

He leads the humble in justice, And He teaches the humble His way.

PSALM 25:9

The Weight of Glory

Scribbling In The Dark

A man can no more diminish God's glory by refusing to worship Him than a lunatic can put out the sun by scribbling the word "darkness" on the wall of his cell.

The heavens are telling of the glory of God; And their expanse is declaring the work of His hands.

PSALM 19:1

The Problem of Pain

Up To No Good

It is funny how mortals always picture us as putting things into their minds: in reality our best work is done by keeping things out.

Put on the full armor of God, that you may be able to stand firm against the schemes of the devil.

EPHESIANS 6:11

One devil to another in *The Screwtape Letters*

The Right Amount Of Evil

There are equal and opposite errors into which our race can fall about devils. One is to disbelieve in their existence. The other is to believe, and to feel an excessive and unhealthy interest in them.

———

...Resist the devil and he will flee from you.

JAMES 4:7

The Screwtape Letters

Dancing Rules

Obedience and rule are more like a dance than a drill.

Through whom we have received grace and apostleship to bring about the obedience of faith...for His name's sake.

ROMANS 1:5

That Hideous Strength

Not Enough Steam

But even the best Christian that ever lived is not acting on his own steam—he is only nourishing or protecting a life he could never have acquired by his own efforts.

I have been crucified with Christ; and it is no longer I who live, but Christ lives in me; and the life which I now live in the flesh I live by faith in the Son of God.

GALATIANS 2:20

Mere Christianity

Gods At High Price

That we, though small, might quiver with
Fire's same
Substantial form as Thou—not
reflect merely
Like lunar angels back to Thee cold flame.
Gods are we, Thou hast said; and we pay
dearly.

---

*I said, "You are gods, And all of you
are sons of the Most High."*

PSALM 82:6

"Scazons" from *Poems*

Did You Know?

He was an outspoken atheist for 18 years of his early career.

**Strong
But
Late**

The things I assert most vigorously are those that I resisted long and accepted late.

...Abhor what is evil; cling to what is good.

ROMANS 12:9

Surprised by Joy

Words Aren't Enough

"I know now, Lord," she said, "why you utter no answer. Before your face questions die away. What other answer would suffice? Only words, words...."

"For My thoughts are not your thoughts, neither are your ways My ways," declares the LORD.

ISAIAH 55:8

Till We Have Faces

Important Interruptions

What one calls the interruptions are precisely one's real life—the life God is sending one day by day: what one calls one's "real life" is a phantom of one's own imagination.

There is an appointed time for everything. And there is a time for every event under heaven.

ECCLESIASTES 3:1

They Stand Together

Paddling Another's Canoe

Others can do for us what we cannot do for ourselves and one can paddle every canoe *except* one's own. That is why Christ's suffering *for us* is...the ultimate law of the spiritual world.

For you have been called for this purpose, since Christ also suffered for you, leaving you an example for you to follow in His steps.

1 PETER 2:21

They Stand Together

A Borrowed Fragrance

Our whole destiny seems to lie in ourselves, in acquiring a fragrance that is not our own but borrowed, in becoming clean mirrors filled with the image of a face that is not ours [but God's].

For we are a fragrance of Christ to God among those who are being saved and among those who are perishing.

2 CORINTHIANS 2:15

"Christianity and Literature" from *Christian Reflections*

Cross Purposes

In every Church, in every institution, there is something which sooner or later works against the very purpose for which it came into existence.

"...upon this rock I will build My church; and the gates of Hades shall not overpower it."

MATTHEW 16:18

Letters to Malcolm

High Pressure Sales

There are people who want to keep our sex instinct inflamed in order to make money out of us. Because, of course, a man with an obsession is a man who has very little sales resistance.

Flee [sexual] *immorality....*
1 CORINTHIANS 6:18

Mere Christianity

Did You Know?

His conversion to Christ was not emotional or even dramatic. He stated "It was more like when a man, after long asleep, still lying motionless in bed, becomes aware that he is now awake."

An Unhappy Convert

That which I greatly feared had at last come upon me. In the Trinity Term of 1929 I gave in, and admitted that God was God, and knelt and prayed: perhaps, that night, the most dejected and reluctant convert in England. I did not then see what is now the most shining and obvious thing; the Divine humility which will accept a convert even on such terms.

...Therefore it says, "God is opposed to the proud, but gives grace to the humble."

JAMES 4:6

Surprised by Joy

Gradual Belief

The Bible itself gives us one short prayer which is suitable for all who are struggling with the beliefs and doctrines. It is: Lord I believe, help Thou my unbelief.

Immediately the boy's father cried out and began saying, "I do believe; help my unbelief."

MARK 9:24

Letters of C.S. Lewis

The Mysterious You

Be sure that the ins and outs of your individuality are no mystery to Him; and one day they will no longer be a mystery to you.

I urge you therefore, brethren, by the mercies of God, to present your bodies a living and holy sacrifice, acceptable to God, which is your spiritual service of worship.

ROMANS 12:1

The Problem of Pain

A Heavenly Fit

Your place in heaven will seem to be made for you and you alone, because you were made for it—made for it stitch by stitch as a glove is made for a hand.

For our citizenship is in heaven, from which also we eagerly wait for a Savior, the Lord Jesus Christ.

PHILIPPIANS 3:20

The Problem of Pain

Ever-Changing Love

In my love for wife or friend the only eternal element is the transforming presence of Love Himself.

———————

Many waters cannot quench love....
SONG OF SOLOMON 8:7

The Four Loves

A Christ-Like Husband

The husband is the head of the wife just in so far as he is to her what Christ is to the Church.

Husbands, love your wives, just as Christ also loved the church and gave Himself up for her.

EPHESIANS 5:25

The Four Loves

God-Chosen Friends

Christ, who said to the disciples, "Ye have not chosen me, but I have chosen you," can truly say to every group of Christian friends, "You have not chosen one another but I have chosen you for one another."

But now God has placed the members, each one of them, in the body, just as He desired.

1 CORINTHIANS 12:18

The Four Loves

Down To The Hour

"Give us our daily bread" (not an annuity for life) applies to spiritual gifts too; the little *daily* support for the *daily* trial. Life has to be taken day by day and hour by hour.

―――――――――

It is written, "Man shall not live on bread alone, but on every word that proceeds out of the mouth of God."

MATTHEW 4:4

Letters of C.S. Lewis

Healed Beyond Medicine

Of course I believe that people are still healed by faith; whether that has happened in any particular case one can't of course say without getting a real doctor who is also a real Christian to go through the whole case-history.

_____

Bless the Lord, O my soul,... who heals all your diseases.

PSALM 103:2-3

Letters of C.S. Lewis

Rules For Prayers

I am certainly unfit to advise anyone else on the devotional life. My own rules are

(1) To make sure that, wherever else they may be placed, the main prayers should *not* be put `last thing at night'.

(2) To avoid introspection in prayers—I mean not to watch one's own mind to see if it is in the right frame, but always to turn the attention outwards to God.

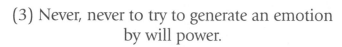

(3) Never, never to try to generate an emotion
by will power.

(4) To pray without words when I am able, but to fall
back on words when tired or otherwise below par.

---

*Seek the LORD and His strength; Seek His face
continually.*

PSALM 105:4

Letters of C.S. Lewis

"Curing" Religion

Keep clear of psychiatrists unless you know that they are also Christians. Otherwise they start with the assumption that your religion is an illusion and try to "cure" it: and this assumption they make not as professional psychologists but as amateur philosophers.

See to it that no one takes you captive through philosophy and empty deception, according to the tradition of men.

COLOSSIANS 2:8

Letters of C.S. Lewis

Did You Know?

Lewis was wounded in action during World War I.

Heavenly Dearest First

When I have learnt to love God better than my earthly dearest, I shall love my earthly dearest better than I do now.

If someone says, "I love God," and hates his brother, he is a liar; for the one who does not love his brother whom he has seen, cannot love God whom he has not seen.

1 JOHN 4:20

Letters of C.S. Lewis

Inventing A Color?

The human mind has no more power of inventing a new value than of planting a new sun in the sky or a new primary colour in the spectrum.

Is there anything of which one might say, "See this, it is new"? Already it has existed for ages which were before us.

ECCLESIASTES 1:10

"The Poison of Subjectivism" in *Christian Reflections*

Think of yourself just as a seed patiently waiting in the earth; waiting to come up a flower in the Gardener's good time, up into the *real* world, the real waking.

A True Awakening

"Truly, truly I say to you, unless a grain of wheat falls into the earth and dies, it remains by itself alone; but if it dies, it bears much fruit."

JOHN 12:24

Letters to an American Lady

The Great Idol Smasher

My idea of God is not a divine idea. It has to be shattered time after time. He shatters it Himself. He is the great iconoclast [idol smasher].

I am the Lord your God...you shall have no other gods before me. You shall not make for yourself an idol.

EXODUS 20:2-4

The Problem of Pain

Passing Into The Beauty

We do not want merely to *see* beauty...we want...to be united with the beauty we see, to pass into it, to receive it unto ourselves, to bathe in it, to become part of it.

One thing I have asked from the LORD, that I shall seek: That I may dwell in the house of the LORD all the days of my life, To behold the beauty of the LORD.

PSALM 27:4

The Weight of Glory

A Zoo Of Problems

For the first time I examined myself with a seriously practical purpose. And there I found what appalled me; a zoo of lusts, a bedlam of ambitions, a nursery of fears, a harem of fondled hatreds. My name was legion.

..."There is none righteous, not even one...there is none who does good."

ROMANS 3:10,12

Surprised by Joy

Love And Marriage

Christianity has glorified marriage more than any other religion: and nearly all the greatest love poetry in the world has been produced by Christians. If anyone says that sex, in itself, is bad, Christianity contradicts him at once.

Let marriage be held in honor among all, and let the marriage bed be undefiled.

HEBREWS 13:4

Mere Christianity

A Dangerous Investment

There is no safe investment. To love at all is to be vulnerable. Love anything, and your heart will certainly be wrung and possibly be broken.

For this is the message which you have heard from the beginning, that we should love one another.

1 JOHN 3:11

The Four Loves

A society which is predominantly Christian will propagate Christianity through its schools: one which is not, will not.

Mainly Christian?

We are destroying speculations and every lofty thing raised up against the knowledge of God, and we are taking every thought captive to the obedience of Christ.

2 CORINTHIANS 10:5

"On the Transmission of Christianity"
from *God in the Dock*

Did You Know?

He initially married his wife, an American, Helen Joy Davidson in a secret civil ceremony to allow her to remain legally in England. Their relationship grew into a deep love.

Causes Of Cruelty

In reality, cruelty does not come from desiring evil as such, but from perverted sexuality, inordinate resentment, or lawless ambition and avarice.

The merciful man does himself good, But the cruel man does himself harm.

PROVERBS 11:17

"Evil and God" from *God in the Dock*

Two Faces Of Ambition

Ambition!...If it means the desire to get ahead of other people...then it is bad. If it means simply wanting to do a thing well, then it is good.

And whatever you do in word or deed, do all in the name of the Lord Jesus, giving thanks through Him to God the Father.

COLOSSIANS 3:17

"Answers to Questions on Christianity" from
God in the Dock

Everybody's Appoint-ment

I find it difficult to keep from laughing when I find people worrying about future destruction of some kind or other. Didn't they know they were going to die anyway? Apparently not.

...it is appointed for men to die once and after this comes judgment.

HEBREWS 9:27

"Cross-Examination" from _God in theDock_

Of What Impor-tance?

Christianity is a statement which, if false, is of *no* importance, and, if true, of infinite importance. The one thing it cannot be is moderately important.

He said to them, "But who do you say that I am?" And Simon Peter answered and said, "Thou art the Christ, the Son of the Living God."

MATTHEW 16:15-16

"Christian Apologetics" from *God in the Dock*

Everlasting Splendours

There are no ordinary people. You have never talked to a mere mortal. Nations, cultures, arts, civilizations—these are mortal, and their life is to us as the life of a gnat. But it is immortals whom we joke with, work with, marry, snub, and exploit—immortal horrors or everlasting splendours.

What is man that you are mindful of him, the son of man that you care for him? You made him a little lower than the heavenly beings and crowned him with glory and honor.

PSALM 8:4-5 NIV

The Weight of Glory

The Early Cobwebs

I am a barbarously early riser...I love the empty, silent, dewy, cobwebby hours.

Morning by morning, O Lord, you hear my voice; morning by morning I lay my requests before you and wait in expectation.

PSALM 5:3 NIV

Letters to an American Lady

Did You Know?

He was a professor of English Literature at both Oxford and Cambridge Universities.

Mere Trifles

We are reluctant to begin. We are delighted to finish. While we are at prayer, but not while we are reading a novel or solving a cross-word puzzle, any trifle is enough to distract us.

———————

Therefore let everyone who is godly pray to you while you may be found....

PSALM 32:6 NIV

Letters to Malcolm

He commands us to do slowly and blunderingly what He could do perfectly and in the twinkling of an eye.

———————

I planted, Apollos watered, but God was causing the growth. So then neither the one who plants nor the one who waters is anything, but God who causes the growth.

1 CORINTHIANS 3:6-7

"The Efficacy of Prayer" from
The World's Last Night and Other Essays

Delegated The Slow Way

Die Now, Live Later

Die before you die. There is no chance after.

———————

It is a trustworthy statement: For if we died with Him, we shall also live with Him.

2 TIMOTHY 2:11

Till We Have Faces

Love's Proper Etiquette

Only the courteous can love, but it is love that makes them courteous.

And beyond all these things put on love, which is the perfect bond of unity.

COLOSSIANS 3:14

The Allegory of Love

Look Outward

We should, I believe, distrust states of mind which turn our attention upon ourselves. Even at our sins we should look no longer than is necessary to know and to repent them; and our virtues or progress (if any) are certainly a dangerous object of contemplation.

Let no man deceive himself. If any man among you thinks that he is wise in this age, let him become foolish that he may become wise.

1 CORINTHIANS 3:18

"Letter to Walter Hooper" from *Letters of C.S. Lewis*

Misery Must End

Either the day must come when joy prevails and all the makers of misery are no longer able to infect it: or else for ever and ever the makers of misery can destroy in others the happiness they reject for themselves.

For the Lamb in the center of the throne shall be their shepherd, and shall guide them to springs of the water of life; and God shall wipe every tear from their eyes.

REVELATION 7:17

The Great Divorce

All And More

He doesn't say that we are to forgive other people's sins provided they are not too frightful, or provided there are extenuating circumstances, or anything of that sort. We are to forgive them all, however spiteful, however mean, however often they are repeated.

"If you forgive the sins of any, their sins have been forgiven them; if you retain the sins of any, they have been retained."

JOHN 20:23

"On Forgiveness" from *Fern-seed and Elephants*

A Natural Offer

All our merely natural activities will be accepted, if they are offered to God, even the humblest: and all of them, even the noblest, will be sinful if they are not.

Whatever you do, work at it with all your heart, as working for the Lord, not for men.

Colossians 3:23 NIV

Learning in War Time

Himself And Everything

"Creatures, I give you yourselves," said the strong, happy voice of Aslan [a lion figure of Christ], "I give to you forever this land of Narnia. I give you the woods, the fruits, the rivers. I give you the stars and I give you myself."

...those who have been called may receive the promise of the eternal inheritance.

HEBREWS 9:15

The Magician's Nephew

A Delicate Man

God could, had He pleased, have been incarnate in a man of iron nerves...[Because] of his great humility He chose to be incarnate in a man of delicate sensibilities who wept at the grave of Lazarus and sweated blood in Gethsemane.

...He has no stately form or majesty that we should look upon Him, Nor appearance that we should be attracted to Him.

ISAIAH 53:2

Letters of C.S. Lewis

To Extremes

He was never regarded as a mere mortal teacher. He did not produce that effect on any of the people who actually met Him. He produced mainly three effects — Hatred — Terror — Adoration. There was no trace of people expressing mild approval.

That at the name of Jesus EVERY KNEE SHOULD BOW, of those who are in heaven, and on earth, and under the earth, and that every tongue should confess that Jesus Christ is Lord....

PHILIPPIANS 2:10-11

"What Are We to Make of Jesus Christ?" from *God in the Dock*

Did You Know?

He was one of the few awarded three first class honors
at Oxford.

Different Paths To Glory

Surely God saves different souls in different ways? To preach instantaneous conversion and eternal security as if they must be the experiences of all who are saved, seems to me very dangerous: the very way to drive some into presumption and others into despair.

For to us God revealed them through the Spirit; for the Spirit searches all things, even the depths of God.

1 CORINTHIANS 2:10

"Letter to Stuart Robinson" from *Letters of C.S. Lewis*

The Face We'll Know

When we see the face of God we shall know that we have always known it. He has...sustained...all our earthly experiences of innocent love. All that was true love in them was, even on earth, far more His than ours, and ours only because His.

For now we see in a mirror dimly, but then face to face; now I know in part, but then I shall know fully just as I also have been fully known.

1 CORINTHIANS 13:12

The Four Loves

God Or A Lunatic?

The idea of a great moral teacher saying what Christ said is out of the question...the only person who can say that sort of thing is either God or a complete lunatic suffering from that form of delusion which underminds the whole mind of man.

While he [Jesus] was still speaking, a bright cloud enveloped them, and a voice from the cloud said, "This is my Son, whom I love...."

MATTHEW 17:5 NIV
"What Are We to Make of Jesus Christ?" from
God in the Dock

Only A Little Knowledge

I sometimes pray not for self-knowledge in general but for just so much self-knowledge at the moment as I can bear and use at the moment; the little daily dose.

Wise men store up knowledge, But with the mouth of the foolish, ruin is at hand.

PROVERBS 10:14

Letters to Malcolm

Reluctant Faith

The young people today are un-Christian because their teachers have been either unwilling or unable to transmit Christianity to them.

"And these words, which I am commanding you today, shall be on your heart; and you shall teach them diligently to your sons and shall talk of them when you sit in your house and when you walk by the way and when you lie down and when you rise up."

DEUTERONOMY 6:6-7

"On the Transmission of Christianity" from
God in the Dock

Earth Belongs Where?

Earth, if chosen instead of Heaven, will turn out to have been, all along, only a region in Hell: and earth, if put second to Heaven, to have been from the beginning a part of Heaven itself.

But the Scripture has shut up all men under sin, that the promise by faith in Jesus Christ might be given to those who believe.

GALATIANS 3:22

The Great Divorce

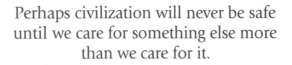

Saving Civiliza-tion

Perhaps civilization will never be safe until we care for something else more than we care for it.

"And you shall love the Lord your God with all your heart, and with all your soul, and with all your mind, and with all your strength."

MARK 12:30

"First and Second Things" from *God in the Dock*

...I never had a selfless thought since I was born. I am mercenary and self-seeking through and through: I want God, you, all friends, merely to serve my turn.

Born Selfish

Do nothing from selfishness or empty conceit, but with humility of mind let each of you regard one another as more important than himself; do not merely look out for your own personal interests, but also for the interests of others.

PHILIPPIANS 2:3-4

"As the Ruin Falls" from *Poems*

Did You Know?

He was a very close friend of J.R.R. Tolkien, author of *The Lord of the Rings*, who was also an Oxford professor.

Pardoned And Excused

To be a Christian means to forgive the inexcusable, because God has forgiven the inexcusable in you.

———

..."Lord, how often shall my brother sin against me and I forgive him? Up to seven times?" Jesus said to him, "I do not say to you, up to seven times, but up to seventy times seven."*

MATTHEW 18:21-22

"On Forgiveness" from *Fern-seed and Elephants*

Waters Of Eternal Life

"I daren't come and drink," said Jill.
"Then you will die of thirst," said the Lion.
"Oh dear!" said Jill, coming another step nearer. "I suppose I must go and look for another stream then."
"There is no other stream," said the Lion.

"But whoever drinks of the water that I shall give him shall never thirst; but the water that I shall give him shall become in him a well of water springing up to eternal life."

JOHN 4:14

The Silver Chair

Happiness Or Correction?

If you think of this world as a place intended simply for our happiness, you find it quite intolerable: think of it as a place of training and correction and it's not so bad.

Beloved, I urge you as aliens and strangers to abstain from fleshly lusts, which wage war against the soul.

1 PETER 2:11

"Answers to Questions on Christianity" from *God in the Dock*

Little Christs

The Church exists for nothing else but to draw men into Christ, to make them little Christs. If they are not doing that, all the cathedrals, clergy, missions, sermons, even the Bible itself, are simply a waste of time. God became Man for no other purpose.

In order that the manifold wisdom of God might now be made known through the church to the rulers and the authorities in the heavenly places.

EPHESIANS 3:10

Mere Christianity

Pride
The
Problem

The Christians are right: it is Pride which has been the chief cause of misery in every nation and every family since the world began.

Pride goes before destruction, And a haughty spirit before stumbling.

PROVERBS 16:18

Mere Christianity

Faculty Thinking

Abstain from all thinking about other people's faults, unless your duties as a teacher or parent make it necessary to think about them.

Therefore let us not judge one another anymore....
ROMANS 14:13

"The Trouble with `X'" from *God in the Dock*

Did You Know?

He was featured on the cover of *Time* magazine as the author
of *The Screwtape Letters*.

Sincerity Is The Key

He will not judge us as if we had no difficulties to overcome. What matters is the sincerity and perseverance of our will to overcome them.

So then, my beloved, just as you have always obeyed, not as in my presence only, but now much more in my absence, work out your salvation with fear and trembling.

PHILIPPIANS 2:12

Mere Christianity

If Christianity is untrue, then no honest man will want to believe it, however helpful it might be: if it is true, every honest man will want to believe it, even if it gives him no help at all.

Honest To God

Jesus said to him, "I am the way, and the truth, and the life; no one comes to the Father, but through Me."

JOHN 14:6

"Man or Rabbit?" from *God in the Dock*

Mud Pies In A Slum

We are half-hearted creatures, fooling about with drink and sex and ambition when infinite joy is offered us, like an ignorant child who wants to go on making mud pies in a slum because he cannot imagine what is meant by the offer of a holiday at the sea. We are far too easily pleased.

And my God shall supply all your needs according to His riches in glory in Christ Jesus.

PHILIPPIANS 4:19

The Weight of Glory

Obey Without Sight

Our [Satan's demons'] cause is never more in danger than when a human, no longer desiring, but still intending, to do our Enemy's will, looks round upon a universe from which every trace of Him seems to have vanished, and asks why he has been forsaken, and still obeys.

Jesus answered and said to him, "If anyone loves Me, he will keep My word; and My Father will love him, and We will come to him, and make Our abode with him."

JOHN 14:23

The Screwtape Letters

A Natural Killer

Christ says, "Give me All. I don't want so much of your time and so much of your money and so much of your work: I want You. I have not come to torment your natural self, but to kill it."

I have been crucified with Christ; and it is no longer I who live, but Christ lives in me....

GALATIANS 2:20

Mere Christianity

Did You Know?

His writings include, but are not limited to, the following areas: children's fiction, literary criticism, adult fiction, poetry, letters, science fiction, apologetics, essays, popular theology, and allegory.

Triangular Thinking

We no more become bad by thinking of badness than we become triangular by thinking about triangles.

Finally, brethren, whatever is true, whatever is honorable, whatever is right, whatever is pure, whatever is lovely, whatever is of good repute...let your mind dwell on these things.

PHILIPPIANS 4:8

A Preface to *Paradise Lost*

*Never
Relevant*

All that is not eternal is eternally
out of date.

———————

...His ways are everlasting.
HABAKKUK 3:6

The Four Loves

Peace and Quiet

We live, in fact, in a world starved for solitude, silence, and privacy: and therefore starved for meditation and true friendship.

———————————

Let my meditation be pleasing to Him; as for me, I shall be glad in the LORD.

PSALM 104:34

Transposition and Other Addresses

Theologians And Christians

One is sometimes (not often) glad not to be a great theologian; one might so easily mistake it for being a good Christian.

I have more insight than all my teachers, For Thy testimonies are my meditation.

PSALM 119:99

Reflections on the Psalms

Solid At Last

We shall be true and everlasting and really divine persons only in Heaven, just as we are, even now, coloured bodies only in the light.

But when the perfect comes, the partial will be done away.

1 CORINTHIANS 13:10

Transposition and Other Addresses

Delighted To Dance

The most valuable thing the Psalms do for me is to express the same delight in God which made David dance.

And David was dancing before the Lord with all his might...

2 SAMUEL 6:14

Reflections on the Psalms

Did You Know?

His book *Mere Christianity* originated from national broadcast talks, when he was a household name in Britain during World War II.

The Dungeon Of Self

...[and] every shutting up of the creature within the dungeon of its own mind—is, in the end, Hell. But Heaven is not a state of mind. Heaven is reality itself.

Then I saw a new heaven and a new earth, because the first heaven and the first earth had passed away.

REVELATION 21:1

The Great Divorce

When all is said…about the divisions of Christendom, there remains, by God's mercy, an enormous common ground.

Grounded Together

"I, Jesus, have sent My angel to testify to you these things for the churches. I am the root and the offspring of David, the bright morning star."

REVELATION 22:16

Preface to *Christian Reflections*

Too Much Translation

Odd, the way the less the Bible is read the more it is translated.

I shall delight in Thy statutes; I shall not forget Thy word.

PSALM 119:16

Letters of C.S. Lewis

An Author In Charge

Some people probably think of the Resurrection as a desperate last moment expedient to save the Hero from a situation which had got out of the Author's control.

For it was the Father's good pleasure for all the fulness to dwell in Him, and through Him to reconcile all things to Himself, having made peace through the blood of His cross...

COLOSSIANS 1:19-20

Miracles

Don't Try Harder

Many things—such as loving, going to sleep, or behaving unaffectedly—are done worst when we try hardest to do them.

Casting all your anxiety upon Him, because He cares for you.

1 PETER 5:7

Studies in Medieval and Renaissance Literature

Brains Included

God is no fonder of intellectual slackers than of any other slackers. If you are thinking of becoming a Christian, I warn you you are embarking on something which is going to take the whole of you, brains and all.

And do not go on presenting the members of your body to sin as instruments of unrighteousness; but present yourselves to God as those alive from the dead, and your members as instruments of righteousness to God.

ROMANS 6:13

Mere Christianity

Mouse Pursues Cat?

Amiable agnostics will talk cheerfully about 'man's search for God'. To me, as I then was, they might as well have talked about the mouse's search for the cat.

The LORD has looked down from heaven upon the sons of men, To see if there are any who understand, who seek after God. They have all turned aside...There is no one who does good, not even one.

PSALM 14:2-3

Surprised by Joy

Did You Know?

After much prayer, his wife was temporarily healed of bone cancer with no medical explanation.

What We Know

Those that hate goodness are sometimes nearer than those that know nothing at all about it and think they have it already.

But God has chosen the foolish things of the world to shame the wise, and God has chosen the weak things of the world to shame the things which are strong...that no man should boast before God.

1 CORINTHIANS 1:27, 29

The Great Divorce

Honor And Shame

"You come of the Lord Adam and the Lady Eve," said Aslan. "And that is both honour enough to erect the head of the poorest beggar, and shame enough to bow the shoulders of the greatest emperor in earth."

Behold, I have found only this, that God made men upright, but they have sought out many devices.

ECCLESIASTES 7:29

Prince Caspian

The glory of God, and, as our only means to glorifying Him, the salvation of human souls, is the real business of life.

The Glory Business

...*"All authority has been given to Me in heaven and on earth. Go therefore and make disciples of all nations, baptizing them in the name of the Father and the Son and the Holy Spirit."*

MATTHEW 28:18-19

"Christianity and Culture" from *Christian Reflections*

Life And Death Faith

You never know how much you really believe anything until its truth or falsehood becomes a matter of life and death to you.

Therefore do not be ashamed of the testimony of our Lord, or of me His prisoner; but join with me in suffering for the gospel according to the power of God.

2 TIMOTHY 1:8

A Grief Observed

You Shall Behold Him

For it is not humanity in the abstract that is to be saved, but you—you, the individual reader, John Stubbs or Janet Smith. Blessed and fortunate creature, your eyes shall behold Him and not another's.

———————

..."*Believe in the Lord Jesus, and you shall be saved.*"

ACTS 16:31

The Problem of Pain

Believe In The Liar

[In Milton's time] men still believed that there really was such a person as Satan, and that he was a liar.

"...[the devil] does not stand in the truth, because there is no truth in him. Whenever he speaks a lie, he speaks from his own nature; for he is a liar, and the father of lies."

JOHN 8:44

A Preface to Paradise Lost

The Same Thing Forgiven

We need to forgive our brother seventy times seven not only for 490 offences but for one offence.

———————

And be kind to one another, tender-hearted, forgiving each other, just as God in Christ also has forgiven you.

Ephesians 4:32

Reflections on the Psalms

Petty Ponderings

The gnat-like cloud of petty anxieties and decisions about the conduct of the next hour have interfered with my prayers more often than any passion or appetite whatever.

The end of all things is at hand; therefore, be of sound judgment and sober spirit for the purpose of prayer.

1 PETER 4:7

The Four Loves

Did You Know?

The 1993 film *Shadowlands* was based upon the relationship of C.S. Lewis with his wife Helen Joy Davidman.

A Wife With Many Hats

A good wife contains so many persons in herself. What was H. [Joy] not to me? She was my daughter and my mother, my pupil and my teacher, my subject and my sovereign; and always, holding all these in solution, my trusty comrade, friend, shipmate, fellow-soldier.

An excellent wife, who can find? For her worth is far above jewels.

PROVERBS 31:10

A Grief Observed

Watch For The Thief

Precisely because we cannot predict the moment, we must be ready at all moments. Our Lord repeated this practical conclusion...watch, is the burden of his advice. I shall come like a thief.

For you yourselves know full well that the day of the Lord will come just like a thief in the night.

1 THESSALONIANS 5:2

The World's Last Night and Other Essays

Desiring Other Worlds

If I find in myself a desire which no experience in this world can satisfy, the most probable explanation is that I was made for another world.

But may it never be that I should boast, except in the cross of our Lord Jesus Christ, through which the world has been crucified to me, and I to the world.

GALATIANS 6:14

Mere Christianity

Political Sickness

A sick society must think much about politics, as a sick man must think much about his digestion.

He it is who reduces rulers to nothing, Who makes the judges of the earth meaningless.

ISAIAH 40:23

The Weight of Glory

Caught In The Act

The surest means of disarming an anger or a lust was to turn your attention from the girl or the insult and start examining the passion itself. The surest way of spoiling a pleasure was to start examining your satisfaction.

Let us examine and probe our ways, and let us return to the LORD.

LAMENTATIONS 3:40

Surprised by Joy

Our Wounded World

When He died in the Wounded World He died not for men, but for each man. If each man had been the only man made, He would have done no less.

...while we were still sinners, Christ died for us.

ROMANS 5:8 NIV

Perelandra

Spiritual Highs And Lows

A Spirit...can be either the best or the worst of created things. It is because Man is...a spiritual animal that he can become either a son of God or a devil.

"And if it is disagreeable in your sight to serve the LORD, choose for yourselves today whom you will serve...but as for me and my house, we will serve the LORD."

JOSHUA 24:15

Miracles

Confused Anger

I maintained that God did not exist. I was also very angry with God for not existing. I was equally angry with Him for creating a world.

For even though they knew God, they did not honor Him as God, or give thanks; but they became futile in their speculations, and their foolish heart was darkened.

ROMANS 1:21

Surprised by Joy

Judgment Above God?

I think that if God forgives us we must forgive ourselves. Otherwise it is almost like setting up ourselves as a higher tribunal [judge] than Him.

If we say we have no sin, we are deceiving ourselves, and the truth is not in us. If we confess our sins, He is faithful and righteous to forgive us our sins and to cleanse us from all unrighteousness.

1 JOHN 1:8-9

Letters of C.S. Lewis

No Right To Happiness

A right to happiness doesn't, for me, make much more sense than a right to be six feet tall, or to have a millionaire for your father, or to get good weather whenever you want to have a picnic.

Every man's way is right in his own eyes, But the LORD weighs the hearts.

PROVERBS 21:2

"We Have No Right to Happiness" from
God in the Dock

Health Nuts

Health is a great blessing, but the moment you make health one of your main, direct objects you start becoming a crank and imagining there is something wrong with you.

For they [my words] are life to those who find them, and health to all their whole body.

PROVERBS 4:22

Mere Christianity

The Birth Of Christ

...Once His life-giving finger touched a woman without passing through the ages of interlocked events. Once the great glove of Nature was taken off His hand. His naked hand touched her. There was of course a unique reason for it. That time He was creating not simply a man but the Man who was to be Himself.

..."The Holy Spirit will come upon you [Mary], and the power of the Most High will overshadow you; and for that reason the holy offspring shall be called the Son of God."

LUKE 1:35

Miracles

The Joy of Indulgence

Virtue—even attempted virtue— brings light; indulgence brings fog.

—————

And by this we know that we have come to know Him, if we keep His commandments.

1 JOHN 2:3

Mere Christianity

Did You Know?

He could quote from memory vast portions of many great classic works of literature.

Humble Wisdom

"And what is this valley called?"
"We call it now simply Wisdom's Valley:
but the oldest maps mark it as the Valley
of Humiliation."

---

*When pride comes, then comes
dishonor, But with the humble
is wisdom.*

PROVERBS 11:2

The Pilgrim's Regress

Answered Beforehand

We have long since agreed that if our prayers are granted at all they are granted from the foundation of the world. God and His acts are not in time.

But do not let this one fact escape your notice, beloved, that with the Lord one day is as a thousand years, and a thousand years as one day.

2 Peter 3:8

Letters to an American Lady

The Vastness Of Prayer

Prayer in the sense of petition, asking for things, is a small part of it; confession and penitence are its threshold, adoration its sanctuary, the presence and vision and enjoyment of God its bread and wine.

"Pray, then, in this way: 'Our father who art in heaven, Hallowed be Thy name. Thy kingdom come. Thy will be done, On earth as it is in heaven. Give us this day our daily bread. And forgive us our debts as we forgive our debtors. And do not lead us into temptation, but deliver us from evil....'"

MATTHEW 6:9-13

"The Efficacy of Prayer" from
The World's Last Night and Other Essays

Sweet For A While

One needs the sweetness to *start* one on the spiritual life but, once started, one must learn to obey God for his own sake, not for the pleasure.

———————

My soul keeps Thy testimonies, and I love them exceedingly.

PSALM 119:167

"The Letters of C.S. Lewis to Arthur Greeves" from *We Stand Together*

Better Left Unsaid

No man who says *I'm as good as you* believes it. He would not say it if he did.

"...there is none who does good, there is not even one."

ROMANS 3:12

The Screwtape Letters

United Forever

Once a man is united to God, how could he not live forever? Once a man is separated from God, what can he do but wither and die?

"Then the King will say to those on His right, 'Come, you who are blessed of My Father, inherit the kingdom prepared for you....' Then He will also say to those on the left, 'Depart from Me, accursed ones, into the eternal fire which has been prepared for the devil and his angels.'"

MATTHEW 25:34,41

Mere Christianity

Give Till It Hurts

I do not believe one can settle how much we ought to give. I am afraid the only safe rule is to give more than we can spare.

"Will a man rob God? Yet you are robbing Me! But you say, 'How have we robbed Thee?' In tithes and offerings."

MALACHI 3:8

Mere Christianity

Peace In Him

God cannot give us a happiness and peace apart from Himself, because it is not there. There is no such thing.

————————

Now may the Lord of peace Himself continually grant you peace in every circumstance. The Lord be with you all!

2 Thessalonians 3:16

Mere Christianity

Heavenly Minded, Earthly Good

If you read history you will find that the Christians who did most for the present world were precisely those who thought most of the next. It is since Christians have largely ceased to think of the other world that they have become so ineffective in this.

And let our people also learn to engage in good deeds to meet pressing needs, that they may not be unfruitful.

TITUS 3:14

Mere Christianity

Heaven —And Earth Too

Aim at heaven and you will get earth thrown in. Aim at earth and you will get neither.

The things you have learned and received and heard and seen in me, practice these things; and the God of peace shall be with you.

PHILIPPIANS 4:9

Mere Christianity

The Slow Trip To Hell

The safest road to Hell is the gradual one—the gentle slope, soft underfoot, without sudden turnings, without milestones, without signposts.

"And do not fear those who kill the body, but are unable to kill the soul; but rather fear Him who is able to destroy both soul and body in hell."

MATTHEW 10:28

The Screwtape Letters

Child-Like Maturity

He [Christ] wants a child's heart, but a grown-up's head. He wants us to be simple, single-minded, affectionate, and teachable, as good children are; but He also wants every bit of intelligence we have to be alert at its job, and in first-class fighting trim.

"Behold, I [Christ] send you out as sheep in the midst of wolves; therefore be shrewd as serpents, and innocent as doves."

MATTHEW 10:16

Mere Christianity

Did You Know?

He was an avid letter writer, and with the assistance of his brother Warnie, replied to hundreds of correspondents regarding many issues.

A *Complete Education*

One of the reasons why it needs no special education to be a Christian is that Christianity is an education itself.

The fear of the LORD is the beginning of knowledge....

PROVERBS 1:7

Mere Christianity

The Grand Choice

You must make your choice. Either this man was, and is, the Son of God; or else a madman or something worse. You can shut Him up for a fool, you can spit at Him and kill Him as a demon, or you can fall at His feet and call Him Lord and God.

...He is Lord of lords and King of kings, and those who are with Him are the called and chosen and faithful.

REVELATION 17:14

Mere Christianity

Present And Accounted For

The great thing is to be found at one's post as a child of God, living each day as though it were our last, but planning as though our world might last a hundred years.

"Take heed, keep on the alert; for you do not know when the appointed time is."

MARK 13:33

God in the Dock

Pain's Mega-phone

God whispers to us in our pleasures, speaks in our conscience, but shouts in our pain: it is His megaphone to rouse a deaf world.

And not only this, but we also exult in our tribulations, knowing that tribulation brings about perseverance; and perseverance, proven character; and proven character, hope.

ROMANS 5:3-4

The Problem of Pain

The Magician's Scam

It is the magician's bargain: give up our souls, get power in return. But...we shall in fact be the slaves and puppets of that to which we have given our souls.

...our old self was crucified with Him, that our body of sin might be done away with, that we should no longer be slaves to sin.

ROMANS 6:6

Mere Christianity

The Larger, Quieter Voice

The moment you wake up each morning, all your wishes and hopes for the day rush at you like wild animals. And the first job each morning consists in shoving it all back; in listening to that other voice, taking that other point of view, letting that other, larger, stronger, quieter life come flowing in.

Rest in the LORD and wait patiently for Him...

PSALM 37:7

Mere Christianity

Look Up Clearly

A proud man is always looking down on things and people; and, of course, as long as you're looking down, you can't see something that's above you.

A man's pride brings him low, but a man of lowly spirit gains honor.

PROVERBS 29:23 NIV

Mere Christianity

Time And Sin

We have a strange illusion that mere time cancels sin....But mere time does nothing either to the fact or to the guilt of sin. The guilt is washed out not by time but by repentance and the blood of Christ.

In Him we have redemption through His blood, the forgiveness of our trespasses, according to the riches of His grace.

EPHESIANS 1:7

The Problem of Pain

Mid-Life Crisis

The long, dull monotonous years of middle-aged prosperity or middle-aged adversity are excellent campaigning weather [for the devil].

Be of sober spirit, be on the alert. Your adversary, the devil, prowls about like a roaring lion, seeking someone to devour.

1 PETER 5:8

The Screwtape Letters

Alive On Arrival

If we really think that home is elsewhere and that this life is a "wandering to find home," why should we not look forward to the arrival?

But according to His promise we are looking for new heavens and a new earth, in which righteousness dwells.

2 PETER 3:13

Did You Know?

His books *Mere Christianity* and *The Screwtape Letters* are still on the best-seller list, and his books have sold in the tens of millions.

Epic Salvation

The salvation of a single soul is more important than the production or preservation of all the epics and tragedies in the world.

_____

"I tell you that in the same way, there will be more joy in heaven over one sinner who repents, than over ninety-nine righteous persons who need no repentance."

LUKE 15:7

Leave It Behind

Has this world been so kind to you that you should leave with regret? There are better things ahead than any we leave behind.

"They are not of the world, even as I am not of the world."

JOHN 17:16

God's Story

History is a story written by the finger of God.

The heavens are yours, and yours also the earth; you founded the world and all that is in it. You created the north and the south.

Psalm 89:11-12 NIV

Whose Thinking?

I read in a periodical the other day that the fundamental thing is how we think of God. By God Himself, it is not! How God thinks of us is not only more important, but infinitely more important.

"For My thoughts are not your thoughts, neither are your ways My ways," declares the LORD.

ISAIAH 55:8

The Weight of Glory

A Good Loss

Every story of conversion is a story of a blessed defeat.

———————

"*Repent therefore and return, that your sins may be wiped away, in order that times of refreshing may come from the presence of the Lord.*"

ACTS 3:19

Another's Possession

I became my own only when I gave myself to Another.

———

"For whoever wishes to save his life shall lose it, but whoever loses his life for My sake, he is the one who will save it."

LUKE 9:24

Letters of C.S. Lewis

Did You Know?

Hc died on the same day that American President John F. Kennedy was assassinated—November 22, 1963.

Other Titles available from The Christian Classics Series
are available from your local bookstore.

C.S. Lewis' Little Instruction Book
A.W. Tozer's Little Instruction Book
Charles Spurgeon's Little Instruction Book
John Wesley's Little Instruction Book
Martin Luther's Little Instruction Book
D.L. Moody's Little Instruction Book

HONOR
BOOKS

Tulsa, Oklahoma